Jupiter

Quinn M. Arnold

CREATIVE EDUCATION
CREATIVE PAPERBACKS

seedlings

Published by Creative Education and Creative Paperbacks
P.O. Box 227, Mankato, Minnesota 56002
Creative Education and Creative Paperbacks
are imprints of The Creative Company
www.thecreativecompany.us

Design by Ellen Huber; production by Joe Kahnke
Art direction by Rita Marshall
Printed in the United States of America

Photographs by Alamy (Janez Volmajer), Art Resource (The
Museum of Fine Arts Budapest/Scala), Corbis (NASA), Getty Images
(Ron Miller/Stocktrek Images), iStockphoto (EnricoAgostoni,
Marina_Poushkina, vjanez), NASA (NASA/JPL, NASA/JPL/DLR,
NASA/JPL/University of Arizona), Newscom (World History
Archive), Science Source (Richard Bizley, Detlev van Ravenswaay),
Shutterstock (Vadim Sadovski, Tristan3D), SuperStock (Nikhilesh
Haval/age fotostock)

Library of Congress Cataloging-in-Publication Data
Names: Arnold, Quinn M., author.
Title: Jupiter / Quinn M. Arnold.
Series: Seedlings.
Includes bibliographical references and index.
Summary: A kindergarten-level introduction to the planet
Jupiter, covering its orbital process, its moons, and such
defining features as its rings, Great Red Spot, and name.
Identifiers: ISBN 978-1-60818-914-4 (hardcover) / ISBN 978-1-
62832-530-0 (pbk) / ISBN 978-1-56660-966-1 (eBook)
This title has been submitted for CIP
processing under LCCN 2017938978.

CCSS: RI.K.1, 2, 3, 4, 5, 6, 7;
RI.1.1, 2, 3, 4, 5, 6, 7; RF.K.1, 3; RF.1.1

First Edition HC 9 8 7 6 5 4 3 2 1
First Edition PBK 9 8 7 6 5 4 3 2 1

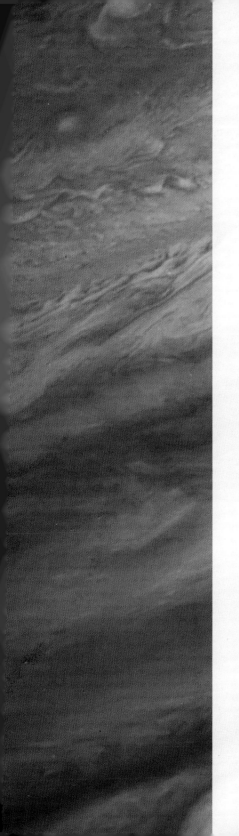

TABLE OF CONTENTS

Hello, Jupiter! 4

Striped Planet 6

Rings and Spots 8

Jupiter's Moons 10

Orbiting Time 12

Discovery Days 14

A Look Inside 16

Goodbye, Jupiter! 18

Picture Jupiter 20

Words to Know 22

Read More 23

Websites 23

Index 24

Hello, Jupiter!

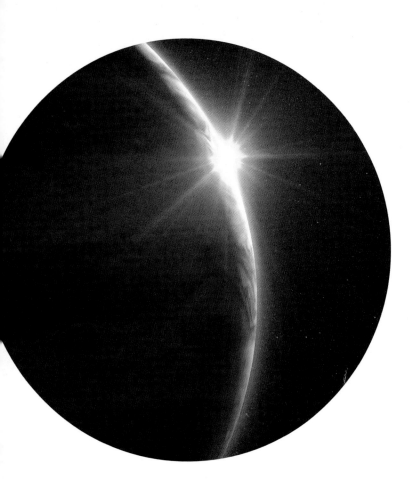

Jupiter is the
fifth planet
from the sun.

Striped Jupiter spins fast. It is cold and windy.

Four dusty
rings circle
Jupiter. They
are hard to see.

A large red spot dots the planet. This is a huge storm. It has lasted for centuries.

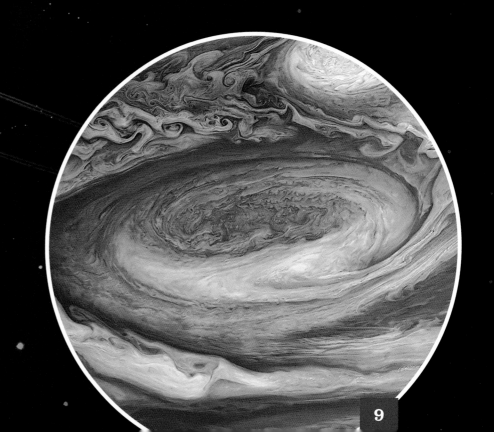

Jupiter has 67 moons! The largest four were found in 1610. They are called the Galilean moons.

Jupiter is the biggest planet in our solar system.

It takes about 12 years to orbit the sun.

Jupiter was found
thousands of years ago.

It was named for an old story about a god. He ruled over all other gods.

Clouds cover the planet. Winds blow. Storms swirl.

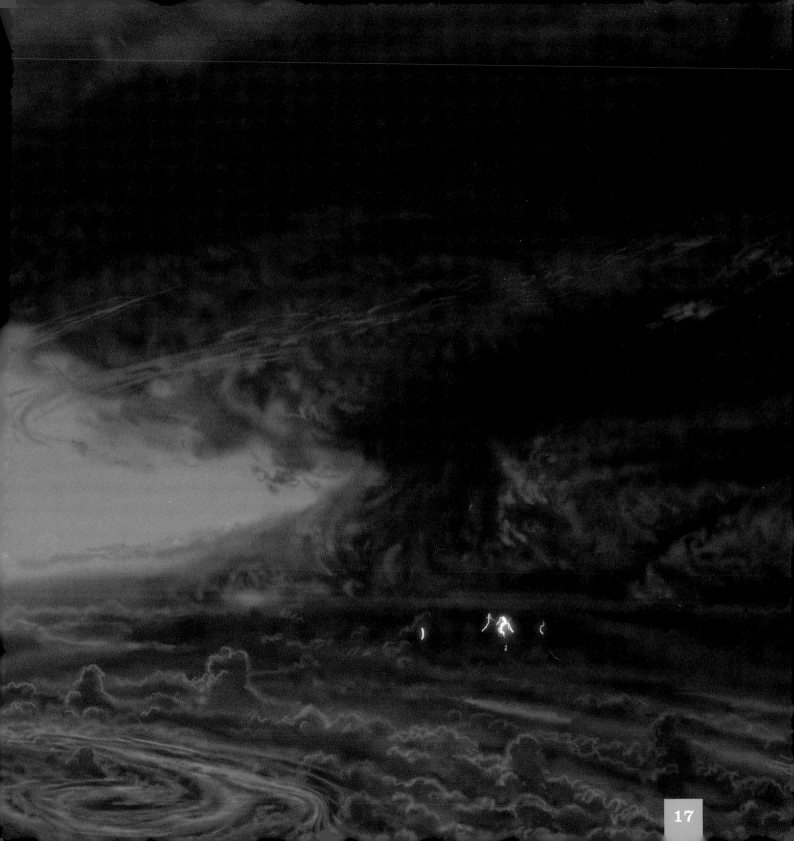

Goodbye, Jupiter!

Picture Jupiter

belts

Europa

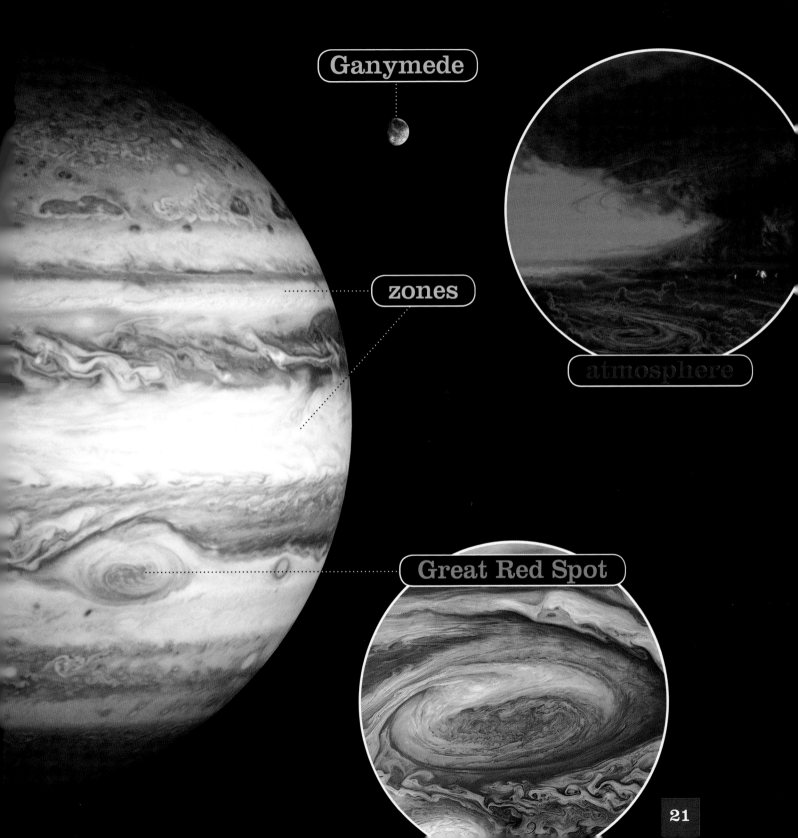

Ganymede

zones

atmosphere

Great Red Spot

Words to Know

centuries: periods of 100 years

god: a being thought to have special powers and control over the world

orbit: the path a planet, moon, or other object takes around something else in outer space

planet: a rounded object that moves around a star

solar system: the sun, the planets, and their moons